# National Parks
# Acadia

**AUDRA WALLACE**

**Children's Press®**
An Imprint of Scholastic Inc.

**Content Consultant**

James Gramann, PhD
Professor, Department of Recreation, Park and Tourism Sciences
Texas A&M University, College Station, Texas

Library of Congress Cataloging-in-Publication Data
Names: Wallace, Audra, author.
Title: Acadia / by Audra Wallace.
Description: New York : Children's Press, 2018. | Series: A true book | Includes bibliographical
    references and index.
Identifiers: LCCN 2017025792 | ISBN 9780531235058 (library binding) | ISBN  9780531238080 (pbk.)
Subjects:  LCSH: Acadia National Park (Me.)—Juvenile literature.Classification: LCC F27.M9 W349
    2018 | DDC 974.1/45—dc23
LC record available at https://lccn.loc.gov/2017025792

All rights reserved. Published in 2018 by Children's Press, an imprint of Scholastic Inc.
Printed in Heshan, China 62

SCHOLASTIC, CHILDREN'S PRESS, A TRUE BOOK™, and associated logos are trademarks and/or
registered trademarks of Scholastic Inc.

Scholastic Inc., 557 Broadway, New York, NY 10012

1 2 3 4 5 6 7 8 9 10 R 27 26 25 24 23 22 21 20 19 18

**Front cover (main): Bass
Harbor Head Lighthouse**
**Front cover (inset): kayaker**
**Back cover: sailboats**

# Find the Truth!

**Everything** you are about to read is true *except* for one of the sentences on this page.

Which one is **TRUE**?

**T or F**   Acadia is one of the largest national parks in the United States.

**T or F**   Giant blocks of ice shaped Acadia's landscape as they moved across the land.

Find the answers in this book.

# Contents

## THE BIG TRUTH!

### National Parks Field Guide: Acadia

Atlantic puffin

Wetlands

# 4 Into the Woods

What types of plants grow in Acadia? . . . . . . . . . . 29

# 5 Preserving the Park

What challenges will Acadia face in the future? . . 35

**Moose**

Until 1918, Cadillac Mountain was called Green Mountain. Its new name honors Antoine Laumet de La Mothe, Sieur de Cadillac, a French explorer.

# A Long History

Acadia National Park is one of our nation's most treasured places. It is often called the crown jewel of Maine. At Acadia, the mountains are closer to the sea than anywhere else on the East Coast. Every fall, people flock to Cadillac Mountain, the park's highest point. They arrive early in the morning, before dawn. From this majestic peak they are the first people in the United States to see the sunrise.

★Acadia National Park

The coast along the Schoodic Peninsula is very rocky.

## Water All Around

Unlike most national parks, Acadia has three separate areas. Part of the park is on the mainland on the Schoodic (SKOO-dik) **Peninsula**. Another part is on a tiny island called Isle au Haut (eye-la-HO). The biggest section is on Mount Desert (duh-ZURT) Island. A bridge connects this island to the mainland. Drive onto a ferry to sail—car and all—to nearby smaller islands. Visitors can also take ranger-led boat tours!

# An Icy Past

Millions of years ago, **glaciers** helped form Acadia's landscape. As the glaciers pushed across the land, they smoothed out the area's rocky mountaintops, making them look like huge scoops of ice cream. They also carved valleys and lakes. They even carried big rocks along with them. Sometimes they dropped the rocks off in odd places. One giant stone called Bubble Rock ended up on the edge of a cliff.

Bubble Rock weighs 100 tons (90.7 metric tons). That is more than 10 times the weight of an elephant!

# People of the Dawn

The first people began arriving in Acadia after the glaciers moved on or melted. For more than 5,000 years, Native American peoples such as the Maliseet, Micmac, Passamaquoddy, and Penobscot lived in the region. Together, these groups are known as the Wabanaki. The Wabanaki hunted animals, gathered berries, and dug for clams along the shore.

# A Timeline of Acadia National Park

## ca. 5000 BCE

**Native Americans settle on the land that is now Acadia National Park.**

## 1604 CE

**French explorer Samuel de Champlain arrives in Acadia.**

# Early Explorers

In the 1500s and 1600s, European explorers arrived in the Acadia area and began mapping it. Over the years, colonists began to settle on Mount Desert Island. They built towns and roads. Acadia later became a popular vacation spot for the wealthy. By the 1900s, overuse of the land's resources, especially its forests, threatened Acadia.

**1913**
John D. Rockefeller Jr. begins construction on the park's famous stone roads and bridges.

**1916**
Acadia is founded as Sieur de Monts National Monument.

**1960**
The number of annual visitors to Acadia tops one million.

**2000**
The park begins restoring and improving its trail system.

# A Park with Many Names

On July 8, 1916, to preserve the area's natural beauty, President Woodrow Wilson set aside a section of Mount Desert Island as Sieur de Monts National Monument. This was done with the help of a group of wealthy nature lovers led by George B. Dorr and John D. Rockefeller Jr. Three years later, the monument became the first national park east of the Mississippi River. It was named Lafayette National Park in honor of the Marquis de Lafayette, a French military leader who supported the United States during the American Revolution (1775–1783). Dorr's group and others continued helping the park grow. In 1929, the park was renamed Acadia, after a French colony formed in the early 1600s in what became Maine.

# National Park Fact File

A national park is land that is protected by the federal government. It is a place of importance to the United States because of its beauty, history, or value to scientists. The U.S. Congress creates a national park by passing a law. Here are some key facts about Acadia National Park.

| Acadia National Park | |
|---|---|
| Location | Maine |
| Year established | 1919 (as Lafayette National Park) |
| Size | More than 47,000 acres (19,020 hectares) |
| Average number of visitors each year | More than 3 million |
| Tallest mountain | Cadillac Mountain, 1,530 feet (466 meters) |
| Deepest lake | Jordan Pond, 150 feet (46 m) |

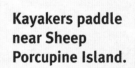

Kayakers paddle near Sheep Porcupine Island.

# Seaside Sights

Beaches are found all around Acadia. Most of them are covered with smooth, round cobblestones. Some cobblestones are as big as basketballs! A few of the beaches, such as the famous Sand Beach, are sandy. But be careful if you go there. There are tiny pieces of sharp, crushed-up shells mixed in with the sand! Other popular attractions at Acadia include Thunder Hole, Otter Cliff, and Somes Sound.

The ocean at Sand Beach tends to be a cool 55 degrees Fahrenheit (13 degrees Celsius) in summer.

The waves that slam into Thunder Hole can splash water 40 feet (12 m) into the air.

## A Thundering Cave

Powerful wind and waves from the Atlantic Ocean constantly batter Acadia's rugged coastlines. This shapes the rock formations along the park's shores. One of the park's most interesting rock formations is a sea cave called Thunder Hole. Part of the cave is underwater. Sometimes wind gets trapped inside. When a big wave smashes into Thunder Hole, the trapped air is forced out. The escaping air sounds like a clap of thunder or loud boom.

# A Beacon of Light

Bass Harbor Head Lighthouse sits high atop the rocks on the southwestern side of Mount Desert Island. It guides sailors into Bass Harbor and Blue Hill Bay. The lighthouse, which stands 32 feet (10 m) high, was built in 1858. Back then, lighthouse keepers climbed to the top of the lighthouse each night to light its oil lamp. Today, the lighthouse is powered by electricity.

# Hold on Tight!

Otter Cliff towers above the waves on Mount Desert Island. At 110 feet (34 m) tall, it is one of the highest cliffs on the Atlantic coast and the tallest in the park. Climbing Otter Cliff is tough. Crashing waves spray the cliff's pink granite walls with water. This makes the rocks very slippery. People hang on to special ropes to get to the top.

Climbers often wear helmets for protection from falling rocks or in case the climber falls when scrambling up Otter Cliff.

A sailboat cuts through the water off the coast of Mount Desert Island.

# Sail Away!

A deep body of water called Somes Sound cuts through the center of Mount Desert Island. Somes Sound is a fjard—a narrow water passage formed by a glacier. It is the only feature of its kind on the Atlantic coast. This waterway is about 5 miles (8 kilometers) long and more than 100 feet (30 m) deep in some spots. Many park visitors travel along Somes Sound in sailboats, canoes, or kayaks.

# CHAPTER 3

# Acadia's Animals

From forests to tide pools, Acadia is known for its variety of **ecosystems**. Each one provides a home for Acadia's many different animals. In the forests, white-tailed deer and snowshoe hares nibble on grass. Beavers build dams in streams, while coyotes and red foxes lurk nearby. Black bears and moose can sometimes be spotted around the Schoodic Peninsula.

 The moose is Maine's state animal.

# At the Water's Edge

When the tide goes out along Acadia's shores, some of the seawater gets left behind in pools between the rocks. Creatures such as dog whelks and sea cucumbers thrive in these tide pools. Sea urchins and periwinkles graze on **algae**. River otters and crabs scamper across thick patches of rockweed while sea stars hunt for mussels to snack on.

Acadia's tide pools are a great place to take an up-close look at the local sea life.

Humpback whales sometimes come very close to the boats that sail by.

## Into the Deep

Out in the ocean, harbor seals and dolphins play in the waves. Humpback whales leap into the air. People go on whale-watching trips on boats for a closer look at them. Some visitors are lucky enough to see Atlantic puffins. These black-and-white birds hang out on small islands in the sea. Their beaks can carry more than a dozen small fish at once!

Don't get too close to snapping turtles—they bite!

## Lake Life

Brook trout, white perch, and about 25 other fish species swim around in the park's lakes and ponds. A few reptiles and amphibians live in the forests nearby. They include snapping turtles, garter snakes, and spotted salamanders. Spring peepers and bullfrogs are busy hopping around, too. These frogs fill the air with their chirps and deep bellowing calls.

# A Bird's Paradise

Acadia is a top spot for bird-watching. More than 300 kinds of birds have been spotted here, including hawks, loons, warblers, and bald eagles. Peregrine falcons also soar overhead. These birds were once in danger of dying out. Acadia's **conservation** efforts helped the falcons bounce back. Today, their nests can be spotted high up in the park's cliffs.

Acadia is known as the warbler capital of North America.

# National Parks Field Guide:
# Acadia

Field guides have helped people identify wildlife and natural objects from birds to rocks for more than 100 years. Guides usually contain details about appearance, common locations, and other basics. Use this field guide to discover six animals you can spot in the park, and learn fascinating facts about each one!

## Atlantic puffin

**Scientific name:** *Fratercula arctica*

**Habitat:** Rocky islands in the North Atlantic Ocean

**Diet:** Fish, crustaceans

**Fact:** This bird is nicknamed the "sea parrot" because of its parrotlike beak.

## North American river otter

**Scientific name:** *Lontra canadensis*

**Habitat:** Ponds, marshes, lakes, rivers, estuaries

**Diet:** Fish, crayfish, crabs, frogs, birds, birds' eggs, reptiles such as turtles

**Fact:** A river otter can run at speeds of up to 15 miles per hour (24 kph) on land.

## Moose

**Scientific name:** *Alces americanus*

**Habitat:** Forests near lakes, rivers, and **wetlands**

**Diet:** Grass, shrubs, moss, **lichen**

**Fact:** This giant deer can swim for several miles across lakes and bays.

## Harbor seal

**Scientific name:** *Phoca vitulina*

**Habitat:** Coastal waters near islands, beaches, and bays

**Diet:** Fish, shellfish, crustaceans

**Fact:** This marine mammal can stay underwater for up to 28 minutes at a time.

## Peregrine falcon

**Scientific name:** *Falco peregrinus*

**Habitat:** A wide variety of habitats, from deserts to mountains, often near coasts

**Diet:** Mostly birds, including ducks and seagulls

**Fact:** A peregrine falcon can dive through the air at more than 200 miles per hour (322 kph) to catch its prey, the fastest speed of any animal.

## Spotted salamander

**Scientific name:** *Ambystoma maculatum*

**Habitat:** Forests, often near rivers and ponds

**Diet:** Small insects, worms, snails, slugs, spiders

**Fact:** This 7-inch-long (18-centimeter) amphibian hides under rocks, logs, and leaves during the day.

# CHAPTER 4

# Into the Woods

Adventure awaits in Acadia's mountains, forests, and wetlands. More than 40 miles (64 km) of stone trails called carriage roads weave through the park. Visitors can hike, bike, and cross-country ski on them. They can even ride in a horse-drawn carriage on the trails. Stone bridges cross over roads, streams, and waterfalls.

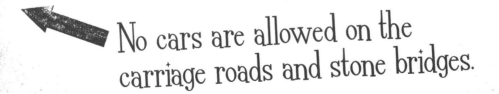

No cars are allowed on the carriage roads and stone bridges.

# Top Trees

Giant **conifers** such as spruce and fir make up most of Acadia's forests. White pines are common, too. These quick-growing coniferous trees can reach more than 100 feet (30 m) tall. Their slender trunks were once used to build masts for ships. **Deciduous** trees such as sugar maples, red oaks, and paper birches are also found in Acadia. Their leaves turn colors in the fall. Lilies of the valley, bunchberries, asters, and goldenrods are among Acadia's more than 800 flowering plants.

Tall trees cover many parts of Acadia.

## Intertidal zones

Clumps of seaweed and moss cling to the rocks along Acadia's shores. Long strands of kelp grow from the ocean floor and sway below the waves.

Kelp

Seaweed

## Wetlands

Partially soaked plants peek out from Acadia's watery bogs, swamps, and marshes.

White water lilies

Cattails

## Forests

A mix of coniferous forests and deciduous forests grows throughout the park.

Sugar maple

Red spruce

## Alpine areas

Plants struggle to survive in Acadia's cold and windy mountains. There is very little soil.

Mountain sandwort

Alpine club moss

# On Soggy Ground

More than 20 percent of Acadia is made up of wetlands. Plants such as white water lilies and cattails grow in the marshes and swamps there. Thick carpets of green, red, and brown moss cover the tops of wet, spongy bogs. Some plants found in the wetlands are in danger of dying out. These rare plants include dwarf rattlesnake root and comb-leaved mermaid weed.

Wetlands are an important habitat for a range of life-forms, including migrating birds and rare plants.

# Master Builder

A wealthy businessman named John D. Rockefeller Jr. was a member of the group that helped create Acadia National Park. Rockefeller donated much of the park's land. In 1913, a few years before the land became Sieur de Monts National Monument, Rockefeller built the carriage roads and stone bridges that now dot the park's landscape. These structures are mostly made of granite cut from Mount Desert Island. Rockefeller wanted them to blend into the natural beauty of the area.

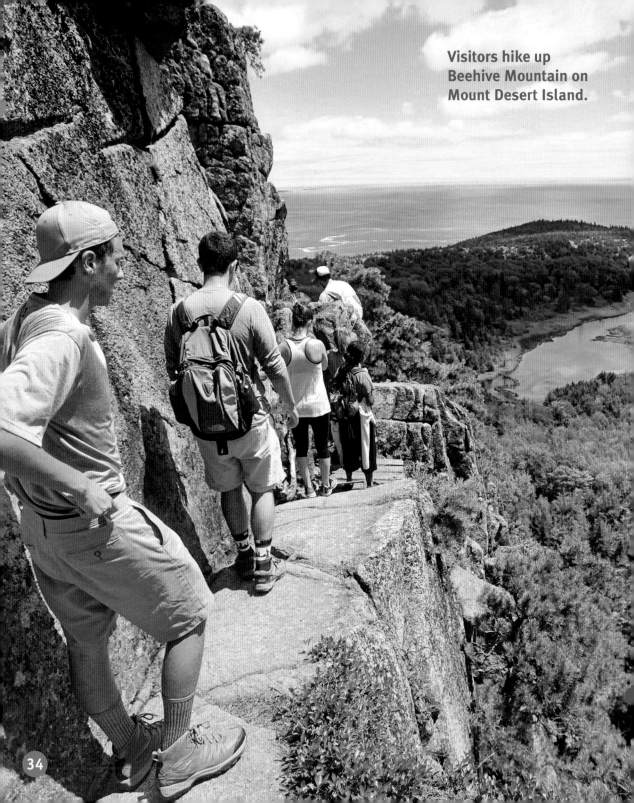

Visitors hike up
Beehive Mountain on
Mount Desert Island.

# CHAPTER 5

# Preserving the Park

Acadia is one of the smallest national parks in the United States. But that doesn't keep more than three million people from visiting it each year. Conserving the park's natural resources is a top priority for the National Park Service. Threats such as **climate** change, erosion, and pollution are constant challenges.

Acadia was the first U.S. national park established east of the Mississippi River.

# Heating Up

Experts have noticed that Maine's climate is changing. They expect the temperature to rise by at least 4 degrees Fahrenheit (7.2 °C) over the next 100 years. Throughout Earth's history, climate change has occurred naturally. However, the use of fuels such as coal and oil is causing this change to happen at a more rapid pace. When those fuels are burned, gases are released into the air. The gases trap heat in Earth's atmosphere.

Long lines of cars are parked along the street near Acadia National Park.

Heavy rains cause erosion that can lead to serious damage to roads and trails in the park.

Climate change may lead to heavier and more frequent rainstorms around Maine. Severe flooding and winds could wipe out the park's delicate coastal ecosystems and further **erode** its rocky shores. Coniferous forests and the animals that live in them may have a tough time surviving. The trees that grow in these forests prefer a cooler climate.

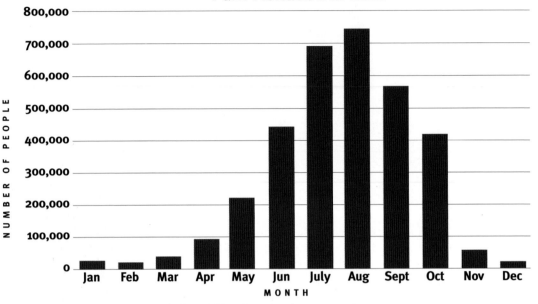

**Park Visitation in 2016**

NUMBER OF PEOPLE

MONTH

Acadia is busiest during the summer.

# Pollution Problem

High levels of air pollution are also a big concern for Acadia. The park is located east of Maine's cities and industrial areas. The cars, trucks, and buildings in these places release harmful gases into the air. Winds from the west blow these gases toward the park. Chemicals in the air even end up in the park's lakes and streams.

## Acadia's Future

As Acadia's popularity grows, the National Park Service is working hard to protect its resources. Park rangers regularly check the air and water to better understand the effects of climate change and pollution on Acadia's ecosystems. Free bus service and new walking trails are in place to limit the amount of cars in the park. The goal is to keep Acadia as wild and beautiful as it was hundreds of years ago. ★

Park visitors gather on top of Cadillac Mountain to watch the sunrise.

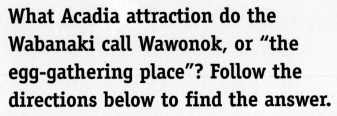

# Map Mystery

What Acadia attraction do the Wabanaki call Wawonok, or "the egg-gathering place"? Follow the directions below to find the answer.

## Directions

1. Start at Acadia's highest peak.

2. Hike southeast to the nearest sandy beach.

3. Travel south to the tallest cliff in the park.

4. You're almost there! Head southwest to the lighthouse at the park's southern tip.

5. Make your way northeast to the narrow fjard that cuts into Mount Desert Island.

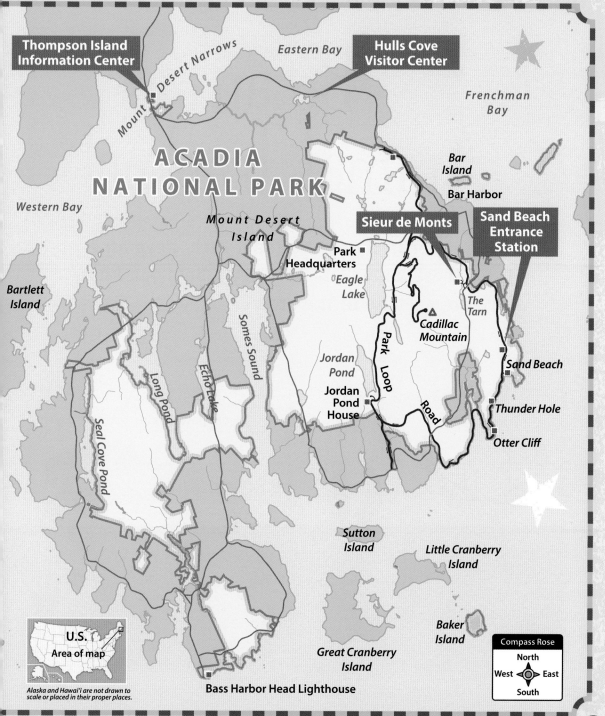

**Thompson Island Information Center**

**Hulls Cove Visitor Center**

*Mount Desert Narrows*

*Eastern Bay*

*Frenchman Bay*

# ACADIA
# NATIONAL PARK

*Western Bay*

*Bar Island*

Bar Harbor

*Mount Desert Island*

**Sieur de Monts**

**Sand Beach Entrance Station**

Park Headquarters

*Eagle Lake*

*Bartlett Island*

*The Tarn*

△

Cadillac Mountain

*Somes Sound*

*Jordan Pond*

Park Loop Road

*Sand Beach*

*Thunder Hole*

*Echo Lake*

Jordan Pond House

*Otter Cliff*

*Long Pond*

*Seal Cove Pond*

*Sutton Island*

*Little Cranberry Island*

U.S.
Area of map

*Baker Island*

**Compass Rose**

North

West 🧭 East

South

*Great Cranberry Island*

Alaska and Hawai'i are not drawn to scale or placed in their proper places.

**Bass Harbor Head Lighthouse**

# Be an Animal Tracker!

If you're ever in Acadia National Park, keep an eye out for these animal tracks. They'll help you know which animals are in the area.

## White-tailed deer

**Hoof length:** 5 inches (12.5 cm)

## Beaver

**Front paw length:** 3 inches (7.5 cm)

## Coyote

**Paw length:** 2.5 inches (6.5 cm)

## Snowshoe hare

**Hind paw length:** 5 inches (12.5 cm)

## Black bear

**Front paw length:** 5 inches (12.5 cm)

## River otter

**Paw length:** 4 inches (10 cm)

**Number of visitors in 2016:** 3,303,393

**Number of mountains:** 26

**Number of lakes and ponds on Mount Desert Island:** 26

**Shortest mountain:** Flying Mountain at 284 ft. (87 m)

**Height of Otter Cliff:** 110 ft. (34 m)

**Height of Bass Harbor Head Lighthouse:** 32 ft. (10 m)

**Length of Somes Sound:** 5 mi. (8 km)

**Number of stone bridges:** 17

**Annual average rainfall:** 48 in. (122 cm)

**Annual average snowfall:** 61 in. (155 cm)

**Average ocean temperature along Acadia's shoreline:** 50° to 60°F (10° to 16°C)

## Did you find the truth?

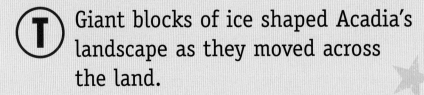

**F** Acadia is one of the largest national parks in the United States.

**T** Giant blocks of ice shaped Acadia's landscape as they moved across the land.

# Resources

## Books

Doak, Robin S. *Maine*. New York: Children's Press, 2018.

Flynn, Sarah Wassner, and Julie Beer. *National Parks Guide U.S.A.* Washington, DC: National Geographic, 2016.

**Visit this Scholastic website for more information on Acadia National Park:**

★ www.factsfornow.scholastic.com
Enter the keyword **Acadia**

# Important Words

**algae** (AL-gee) small plantlike organisms without roots or stems that grow in water or on damp surfaces

**climate** (KLYE-mit) the weather typical of a place over a long period of time

**conifers** (KAH-nuh-furz) evergreen trees that produce seeds in cones

**conservation** (kahn-sur-VAY-shuhn) the protection of valuable resources, especially wildlife and plants

**deciduous** (de-SIJ-oo-uhs) shedding all leaves every year in the fall

**ecosystems** (EE-koh-sis-tuhmz) all the living things in a place and their relation to their environment

**erode** (i-ROHD) wear down

**glaciers** (GLAY-shurz) slow-moving masses of ice found in mountain valleys or polar regions

**lichen** (LYE-kuhn) a flat, mosslike growth often found on rocks and trees

**peninsula** (puh-NIN-suh-luh) a piece of land that sticks out from a larger landmass and is almost completely surrounded by water

**wetlands** (WET-landz) areas where there is a lot of moisture in the soil

# Index

Page numbers in **bold** indicate illustrations.

# About the Author

Audra Wallace graduated from Ithaca College, where she studied film production and elementary education. Her passion for writing nonfiction and teaching kids led her to a position with Scholastic. Since 2006, Wallace has written and edited the award-winning classroom magazine *Scholastic News* Edition 3. She and her family enjoy exploring the great outdoors near their home in New York—and beyond!